THE BESTIARY

Dennis Cooley

TURNSTONE PRESS

The Bestiary

Turnstone Press
Artspace Building
206-100 Arthur Street
Winnipeg, MB
R3B 1H3 Canada
www.TurnstonePress.com

Turnstone Press gratefully acknowledges the assistance of the Canada Council for the Arts, the Manitoba Arts Council, the Government of Canada through the Canada Book Fund, and the Province of Manitoba through the Book Publishing Tax Credit and the Book Publisher Marketing Assistance Program.

Some of this material has appeared in other versions in *CV2*; *RKology*, Ed. Dawne McCance; *correction line*; *Jacket2*; *Stanzas*; *Winnipeg Free Press*; *The Society*; *Shaping a World Already Made* by Carl J. Tracie; *A/Cross Sections: New Manitoba Writing*, Eds. Katherine Bitney and Andris Taskans.

Cover Image: Sterling Clavelle
Interior Images: Gail Trussler

Printed and bound in Canada.

Library and Archives Canada Cataloguing in Publication

Library and Archives Canada Cataloguing in Publication
Title: The bestiary / Dennis Cooley.
Names: Cooley, Dennis, 1944- author.
Description: Poems.
Identifiers: Canadiana (print) 20190233729 | Canadiana (ebook) 20190233737 | ISBN 9780888016690 (softcover) | ISBN 9780888016706 (EPUB) | ISBN 9780888016713 (Kindle) | ISBN 9780888016720 (PDF)
Classification: LCC PS8555.O575 B47 2020 | DDC C811/.54—dc23

MIX
Paper from responsible sources
FSC® C103567

THE BESTIARY

More Poetry by Dennis Cooley

this only home

seeing red

Irene

the stones

departures

to Robert Kroetsch—who he was, what he wrote.
Thanks to Diane Cooley, her constant support, and
Rob Budde, wise and patient reader.

Contents

"A Prairie Boy's Eden"

THE FROGS

THE CROW

THE SPIDER

ARKOLOGY

THE BIRDS

THE BESTIARY

"A Prairie Boy's Eden"

Once upon a time in the village of Heisler—

—Hey, wait a minute.
That's a story.

—Robert Kroetsch, *Seed Catalogue*

near the door

a crumpled towel
a ball of yarn

yawns and rises
he has been visiting eternity

ambushes those who greet or pass
OWWW ooww **OOWW**
calls to those who enter

now now
now he cries
when some one
steps through

NEW NEW the cat calls
has read the writing on the floor
he has something to tell them
something to say

[makeitnew makeitnew]

now he croons
it's now or never

you've got to make it new
you've got to make it now
's the time here
's your chance what
's your line now
's the time

behold the gophers

do they not whistle
in the hot & crinkled air

squeaky words to the wind & the dust
do they not now nod & bow
their large dark eyes
now as always
when we raise
our arms
& the winds
blow hotly

bird of omen

NAW

crow pleads her case
she has seen enough
she has heard the voices
writhing in air

splendid with rejoinder
crow digs in & hollers
fills her lungs & streaks
messages over the sky

naw naw

when the wind rips
earth open crow
lugs her findings home
inside her braggadocio voice
tugs & admires her black leggings

she likes the sound when she drags
her toenails across the blue slate
and with a loud crack it fractures

as for that

consider where   she stands
among   cinders & gravel
her shoulders   shredding wind
she is not   satisfied merely to
return
the world's summons

you have seen her
swagger past   a barn full of cats
& admire   her own
brittle toenails
spend days in their   contemplation

the water's edge

could be you
are looking for something
in the oats & the flax
ducks in their waxy squabbles and frogs
splunk into the soupy green

: splop sblloop

making up for lost time
and most of all crow's
black-beaked gibes

making hay

look also to the lowly grasshopper
does she not say yes in every leap

when she scratches initials in your ear
does she not in her speaking dent
the hot and flowing sun

does she regard every blade of grass
she kneels before & rises from
rattly with thanks

grateful as a logger in the black
forest dreaming sawmills in formosa, ontario
wheat fields under the oil of leduc, alberta

george

his symphony a zoo

pigs camels parrots foxes birds cats mice monkeys
take turns quarreling in your throat

they dislodge chirks and chirrs (plaintive & contented)
when you scrabble across the floor, screams
in fear, outrage, leave-me-alone snit

sprawled in sleep on your back
slumped into your loose skin
you cannot stop the dieselings
or end the simpers

a menagerie possesses you
when you follow your nose to the screen door
hisses and snorts open your mouth
until you choke and groan and
out come a cacophony of clucks and scoldings

your days fill up with wolves   sheep   motors
a macédoine of horns
buzzers , whistles , rumblings ,

there are blue jays mourning doves budgies
strange creatures whose yips and gibbers
you can never exorcise or contain
the squeals of pigs whimpers of dogs
have moved in and you are occupied
by snuffs and clicks and howls

you stage night raids, day-time too
romancing grapes and sausage
the headfirst plunge into the fridge

in shrill & bluster inspect
what i read and what i write carefully
squat & with bookreviewerly zeal
shit upon

they talk

HHRRRHHHRRHRH HGHRRUHH
i call to my friend
who has hefted me
upon the magic of a plank
sprung me loose
to hough and huckle

crippled old boar
from arthritis righted
that I might snort and snork
i have been lifted
that I might feed
and we might
greet one another

RRHRHHRR HGHRR he says
and i the same in meeting
lift my splendid chin
hhrrhh **hhruhh**

we pick up where we left off
we carry on like that all summer

his dad pleased
when he gets wind of this
the two of us by the pumphouse

first quiet and then
wondering grin will

shake his head

you could swear
you were talking
he will say

the owl is the only bird

owls install
their calls in the cold
in small still hearts
chilled with snow

the owl is a bowl
open as the moon is round
its call a wound
that uncorks night
its unspoken sorrow

stands on darkness, sieves
the air we breathe through its mouth
the rustle, over snowy stubble

a handful of vowels,
a pocket full of consonants
wet air between

owl in its house
speaks small things

leaves   and returns
its mate   its young

some times talking
to itself speaking
elisions into the blind fields

afloat in a bowl
owl glides easily to the meeting
the cries of those
who do not hear
and are deathly stricken

arrived from somewhere

suddenly /

before one year they were gone

high in the corner
two white pigeons gaze
down into the box of sun
dust floats sweetly in
and in winter cold

perfectly still when he shines
the flashlight into their eyes
and he carries their softness
tenderly through the winter night
into the house

their eyes still watch
when his cousin Garry
who will die a few years
later of leukemia
falls in the loft and a nail
pokes him in the eye

mar 8

crow is muscling in from the south
mid-march and off course
into a wall-hard wind at 20
below rides the wooden will of his faith
scratches the match in his brain on the 49th

/one lone crow
summoned to summer
will take away the sting of winter

wears wind at night
/heroically
round his neck

gulps till he is two
sheets to the wind
and has dragged the night
into himself the darkness
inside his eyes scratches
his inner ear until
he is scraped clean

crow bitter with vision
realizes in some dim way
the snow will always howl
across the aluminum prairie

when the world rolls into sight
this is all crow can know of
the recent & sun-burnt sky
the wind-chilled earth

sat in front of

the wooden cabinet leaking music
leaking the farm a pale blue

'54 plymouth over the hill
he was 12 or 11 his father was
sunburned & his mother knew
the animals lived next
to their skin & a neighbour
shot himself **blam**
fell into a kid's terror
they called a slough

the cats yawning dark
drank morning on hind legs
milk sprayed from the teats ate
mice squashed to death the cows stepped
or lay on the dog ate frozen shit the rats ate
chop the kid ate the cows ate the dog

their heads off red feathers jumped at the end of the clothes
hanger the garter snake slithered through their nests the cold
seized the kid under the lantern shook the shadows that listened
and brushed the tar paper

the coldmoon horns
the loud shout
his father sudden
at the door
the monocled moon

at the dugout

when we spotted it
escaped from the bank
a whip in the backbone

head high as the Queen of Siam herself
and brazen with stripes
as if she had fled all the way from Salem
to sloughs miasmal with algae

swift muscle when it swims
skims the dugout
quick & finicky
unlaces the water
in a necklace of bright beads

El Greco barking Steve
throwing clumps of gumbo
/ shouting

the sarus crane

a tall stately thing
slim as smoke, clean as slate

an elegant house of sticks
balances delicately
        outstretched
                                        & bowing
                                          leaping into

the bouncing air
the sticks it throws
& in its beak catches

a big booming voice
5 feet long
always in touch

a dance to
please his lady

scriptorium

the gulls gorging themselves
        follow the tractor
in cursive script
        curl the earth
listen for the sounds

machines scraping winter off
the discer   the cultivator   the one-way
        through pillars of dust
                writing one way
                                & then
                        the other

        verses & reversings
                incise the earth
every spring emendations
                reinvent the fields
the windy sweep of estevan

                                the birdhigh voices
                                descant to a plain song
                                shadow him

                                the pages re:
                                        arranging when
                                he turns them and
                                        they darken

        his hand inscribes the earth the
        coming & going
        strange letters in the dirt
        the wind & weeds will soon erase

jumped-up threads

black nibs
prepared to incant can
ticles to light the sun twitch
in italics write
strange language on water
mmmmmmm
mnnnmmm

flash & sing
like sewing machines
stitching the ditches together

through the thickness of heat
embroider the water
they walk on

all day & all night
the high keening
in ecstasy stings
the water's skin

the locusts
(their locus)

pianissimo

heel & toe on their silk
stockings their black finery
string beads on hot filaments
their shaky soprano
italian opera stars gone
dark & sweaty
vicious in the viscous heat

starved widows
on winter rations their
terrible cries at the windows
the squeezed & tweezered voices
reset the season's ratios

heirs apparent they are
bristly at yr gramma's nostrils
hairs in her blood lines

they put on airs
sew sequins on
summer they do fine

needle work knit scarves
speak in bloody non sequiturs
persist in sans serif

swim within their black fish bones
smoke stuck in their throats

on top of the hill (for my father, what he told me)

a long spine locked the hill in place
rocks in two lines of vertebrae
a huge buffalo sleeping
inside a hide of wolf
willow and buffalo

grass snow in april rotted
clumps in the hollows
the ravine in spring ran cold
with water his cousin fell in
ran with reeds and muskrats
someone ran and killed

            across the road
where he found a bone arrow
head the kid standing and standing
inside the fence beside a vixen
and her pups who played at night
someone stood and killed
and the boys splattered
frogs to death with a 22

his eyes reaching until he must
see the whole world and all the holes
in it or the den beside

once must have been a vast grass
field a fox ran through, red flame
the world received so impossible so silent

must have felt and held
their breath where he stands
against the wind mile after mile
sky so forever they felt their eyes
tearing up in wind the earlier people
their ears like his loud with it

sun and grass and wind yea high
the earth sprinkled with crocus
studded with graves, people
breathing inside the hill

Hetty

an old hen /barred
rock they called Hetty
Ms. Hen Rietta Lamour
and she was slow and lame

also dingy among
the persnickety birds
the hennaed chickens
that mince & fluff
in near disdain pick over the jewels

all day she scratched for a revelation
under a glowering sun
lowered herself daintily
into the powdered dirt
flapped it like talcum around her

appeared at my aunt's
        from a secret
                                nest late
                        last fall four
yellow dandelions behind her
the air stinky with burning grass
peeping their way to death

for some reason had also sat
        steadfast in brooding
                        on a clutch of turkey eggs
spread herself like a contagion
                                over their hugeness

found as she must & must not
have expected days
later five puffs of gray
whose faltering she pecked
                & fretted over
                pawkkk pockpockpock

one a penny
two a penny
and soon fell behind

    a mother's worry
when they rose from her
like beans in spring hurried
their long-necked hunger past
her short legs into the yard
twitching with bugs & scratches

every evening brought their red
rubber necks back to her
ducked & tucked close to
her small nervous head

her dusty hen smell
their soft bird sounds of meeting

the small memory

is his gramma
at a table a silver thimble a linen sampler
& an empty cup

a simple basket
& in it oranges & lemons
small sour suns
their bumps & nipples

a teapot-brown table (maple)
once black
once his grandmother's
warm in sun

and on it 30
years later a
coffee cup its handle
a looped shadow

an old lady time blows by
tall at 92 as she could be
the small wells
worn into the stairs
memory a cyst in her
palm flickers across the chairs
the table's welts and scratches
and one deep gouge

all summer
bright spores drift over the wood
the window shining

the small memory is his gramma bent
her silver fingers stiff & knuckled

beside the cup a
silk thread
the exquisite
corpse of a mosquito

a time to harvest

While the earth remaineth, seedtime and harvest,
and cold and heat, and summer and winter,
and day and night shall not cease.

august. an auger. augury. the world's injuries.
a flurry in air. a sudden crash—
the haemorrhage of lights

clack & suck the great red cupboard the straw talk warm fields
blink into a mason-jar moon a bloodeyed ark shucks rabbits
swallows ducks weasels mice small birds feathers & fur on a belt

the lip of dark spills torn things
their clucks & barks & muffled cries

his family a hunger in him
the bread in the swath
the unravelling of warm bodies

the sky rears and shudders to dust to dust the edges roaring
the huge machine rattles he shouts to hold the noise his sudden
breath the air chopping inside the sack of dust the man in goggles
lifting his face the sting in his eyes a snowfall of chaff a fuzzy halo
of light

small mangled creatures
scream when they embark
creatures torn from the ark
returning to the wet & the dark

king of the beasts

It's early August, Regina. I'm a young fellow in from the farm. Tate—our farm was at Tate. I have a dollar, maybe a dollar twenty-five, and there was this lion. There weren't many people on the grounds but this barker was saying The King of Beasts, Step Up and See the King of Beasts. And so I paid my quarter and I climbed up the metal stairs, there were about twelve of them, up onto this platform.

And then there was a ring, a big cage in the middle and it was the King of Beasts, he was big. There was a catwalk all the way around the cage, you were back from here to the cupboards. This lion walks all the way around the edge of the cage, once. And then he stops. He stops right in front of me. He turns his rear end toward me and looks back over his shoulder at me.

And then—psstt—he lets me have it, a quart of it, soaks me while I'm standing there.

It was a very hot day in August, I'm in from the farm, and I'm drenched by the lion.

I just left. I didn't even ask for my quarter back, I just left.

the souris

the 3 jack 2 small 1 larger his grampa
wilson pulls   38 years   out of the souris
slow bend   at Possum's   his wager

            he would find
the filtered light a muddy bank
even then   must have been
sour with heat and sludge   though he
remembers it as   sweet
the bank   as grass

the slow   suspicion on the chain
the day   forms in water
the float &   darkgreen
mucous of their buoyance

sun nets—frogs, fish,
river, a grampa, a boy—

the place where it begins
to spool in strings
astringent with memory

on the bank they   gasp
where they have   pulled them
from the water they cannot   see
far into but   feel
the heft in   their hands
the long slippery
music of their lives

their valves   yanked
3 jacks in the trunk   leak
their lives into   tires & wrenches

the green speckles
gulp &   fill up on air
flop in the dust

the crunch of gravel
into   sudden darkness
roll   the big black
car   dust sifting
grittily   from the fenders
the smell   of gasoline
in the air   the car   the upholstery
the garbage of heat   & corks

grampa and boy   to the stucco house
his gramma lies within   her broken hip
her wax ears   watch
the curtains return   to dust
the cups   on the cupboard
they will   drink tea from

later/
preparing supper
the shallow basin
one of the   little ones
starts   swimming

sparrows

the ragweed stiffens
in wind nothing but
sparrows at their music
prick the days
the trampled snow
paths we do not
step off
nothing but sparrows
on the wires
chirp & twitter of

storm staid

horses in storm hold their tails
        between their legs

draw back into themselves
when he tosses the blanket
        across their backs
hitched against the january cold

wet snow on their faces
        eyelashes freezing

cattle hunch and shiver
        slurp heavily at the barrel

suck down the icecold
        water in long painful gulps

release their warmth
        in thin lumps of ether

stiff-legged & huffing
        back to the barn

winter window

light draining from the portholes
        smoke from the roof exhaling

the farm is
        drifting across the prairie
                winter on the front steps, lurking
the slow sounds of creatures inside

cattle at the haystacks
        huddle together
          wait under the night

        the sky a huge thing
stars become stowaways stare brightly
                    earth tucked under

a snow-white winter
        we lie in
              and forever under

the farm is letting out
        its breath or catching
              sparrows from its blowhole

the creatures

you've got to remember
your Ps and Qs
all the glitches in our plans
the years of itches & clichés
the geese queuing
the ditches chowdered with tadpoles
you would have sworn

frogs were emeralds and they shone
saskatoons sharpened on sun
turned to tart & gooseberries
screwed up on their spindly legs
berries swollen so large and pale a person
could almost see through

there also was the cow called Esmeralda
whose hormones blew past
a ruddy and sometimes luminous moon

and sandhill cranes would wade
the hills in quadrille and the prairie
chickens ran thickly in front
of the chilled morning

they square-danced and dosey-doed
high-stepped in front of the old truck
almost stopped the stupid things
dead in their tracks and coyotes
coaxed the moon from their throats

a time when
potatoes rolled out of the ground
big as cabbages round
as groundhogs the rain
fell hard or softly

found the just and the un
just in the Souris
Valley and on the fields
of France pulled january

across the cold
foxes trotted over
the sheets we pulled
over our breath
quick to give and find
where they left their tracks

and do you dream the secret hay
the smell of flowers
when you let yourself back
into the soft dust
its tea and yielding

        spring summer winter fall
        the moon cracked open
        leaked marrow over
        our upturned faces

THE FROGS

And it is not only the frog that frequents ponds and streams that is thus injurious to them, but the bramble-frog as well, which will come to the hives even in search of them, and crawling up to the entrance, breathe through the apertures; upon hearing which, a deep booming made resonant by the frog's beating upon the hive, a bee flies to the spot, and is snapped up in an instant.

—Pliny the Elder, *Natural History: A Selection*.
Trans. John F. Healy

amphibian love

the leopard frog

has a lot of calls
to make: one

is supposed to attract
females and other males to a

breeding pond; another is given
by a male when he is seized (mis

takenly) by another; and a third
call (a rising gasp) is uttered

by a male just before he
grasps a female; a fourth kind

is made only by the female
when she definitely is

not interested

taking soundings

until we strangle
on our own shadows
stoop and scoop frogs
glimmering bars of soap

slip from our grip
in ditches unspool
turn into pearls in small bottles
filled with champagne
pale & cold they
shine in the hand
purl at our ankles

fizz their lives away
in woozy weather

sometimes they are stars
always they are night
jars & some
times fog horns

& sometimes they are
wet silk hung in the ozone
parachutes caught
on loose rain

their throats thread moons

toads on their
wrinkled thumbs tread
slowly smug
gle leaves & shove mud

their small brains
hunch under a silver & bulbous moon
burn under clusters of light
one large diamond
embedded in their heads

the cold in our throats
where we bend

far as the milky way
a high frequency
the frogs
shiver when they blow
into the night

consummation

something is trying
to organize the night

we lie inside
letters to be sent

meant for
somewhere someone

to unfasten the screen
door to the morning

spiders swing
from the doorknobs

hoist the curtains
the frog's panicked calls

an opera in the slough
their bubble eyes blink
fly and egg

a sticky mess
a cloudy rapture

THE CROW

She saw a bird. And then she counted nine,
All talking crows, complaining in high voices—
Which imitate whatever noise they choose—
Of their sad fate. Minerva seemed surprised.

—Ovid, *The Metamorphoses*, Book V.
Trans. Horace Gregory.

crow creates earth

scans the mud
she will call earth
wherever she spits
saliva glistens & pockmarks

crow watches the caribbean turn electric blue
tilts on her toes tints the days vermillion
smears them in chartreuse in cyan in rust
fills in cobalt & ochre indigo & goldenrod
adds woad & madder slate & ruby
daubs cadmium & manganese blue in burnt umber

in the coal-blue cold crow compresses until
her heart becomes so clear it cannot be
marked & will not break
gulps the raw new light
flings the stars over her shoulder
pins them onto the pewter moon

cries out when she turns
back hears the spinning
gasps when she sees the blue
& white world for the first time
so bright & wetly shining

yeah

y e a h   yeah
she has eaten night
                              what of it
what are we going to do
                                                    about it

there's no two ways about it
it sticks in her craw
it makes her good
                    & sick

        to hear us talk
makes her sick to the stomach

she has had it up to here
& if it was up to her

here's what she wld say

in black & white

columns   keys
costume   customs
crow hunkers down in vast
sheets of parking lots
kicks at the fast-food litter
the snow in its dirty coarseness
scabs of ice the colour of slag

crow whistles & cracks his knuckles
blows on his toes
sucks on his lozenge heart
hopes one day
to sing
country grand ole
opry blue grass rhythm
& blues in rasp
berry grit a wild
& incomparable timbre

his big voice
belting gospel
in stirring four
part harmony

in a dead branch

a congregation of cows watch
from their gentle astonishment

so credulous they chew their cuds
let loose a halo of moos

four small moons
float luminously

over the evening
up to the crows

as the crow flies

back & forth   b l a c k & f o r t hh
back & forth   b l a c k & f o r t hh
back & forth   b l a c k & f o r t hhback
& forth   b l a c k & f o r t hhback &
forth   b l a c k & f o r t hhback & forth
b l a c k & f o r t hhback & forth   b l a c
k & f o r t hhback & forth   b l a c k &
f o r t hh

f b hh back o a & f t o a forth o & b r b k r & & & k t forth r c r
c a t a c hhback t l & r t hh back forth r o b forth & & hhback o
& & o l o r b & f r forth hhback & r f hhback r o b & hh back t
& hh back l f o b k & forth forth a b o o c l b o & r hhback & o
& t a c l hhback & forth b forth forth hh back

f hhback t t a t f b c o f f o c f & l l o l f l a f f hhback hh back a
forth c r t a c o r & o a o back & a l r l & l c r forth a t hhback o
c a r t o forth c f r c l t & c k k b f l l forth r f t forth a t forth &
a b k r o k f k o k c forth hhback & l b hhback f f t &

is a victorian schoolmaster

fancies himself in funereal threads
grimness stiffens his robes
shine where he has rubbed

                            ttsskk tskkk a grim taskmaster
        brisks to the ledge
                                   one swift pass
                                sideswipes winter
                            / swipes the board clean

      crow sneezes on the dust
raises his voice at those who show up
                    in bright duds & come
                    much too late sing much
                  too happily crow knows
      loneliness has made him cruel

crow has standards to uphold
knows they should not let
out a peep when he stands
lugubrious as tar & speaks
in a strong esophageal voice
disquisitions on pens & pinions
his words aureate and resounding

in calvinist clothes encloses himself
swells up big as a cow in calving

crow loves the smell of his own must
      his cellared and collared opinions

                            every night before he
                            disappears into his talk he
                            practices on his boney knees

alone & in his room he loves
to pirouette on cold & squeaky feet

crow gets cold

gets old
gets cold

the sky full of lacerations
crow feels inconsolably blue
and irretrievably lost

a mere wink, blackest smudge
on a staring and vacant sky

crow feels slow as fudge
huddles into a dirty scarf
scowls across a prairie
rutted with badgers
and stiff-necked winds

fears the cold density of night
will compress him to iridescence
crow watches night grind stars off the wind
contemplates Magellan at the cape
witches bright lights at bonfires

wonders why he himself no more
than a housefly
on a parchment world
must scuff why
wade through scruffy skies
cling to a tubercular moon
sing in his rubber boots

THE SPIDER

And as she turned away she sprayed her features
With droppings from dark herbs of Hecate;
Hair, ears, and nose fell off, the head diminished,
The body shrivelled, and her quick long fingers
Grew to its sides with which she crept abroad–
All else was belly, and the girl a spider,
The tenuous weaver of an ancient craft.

—Ovid, *The Metamorphoses*, Book VI.
Trans. Horace Gregory.

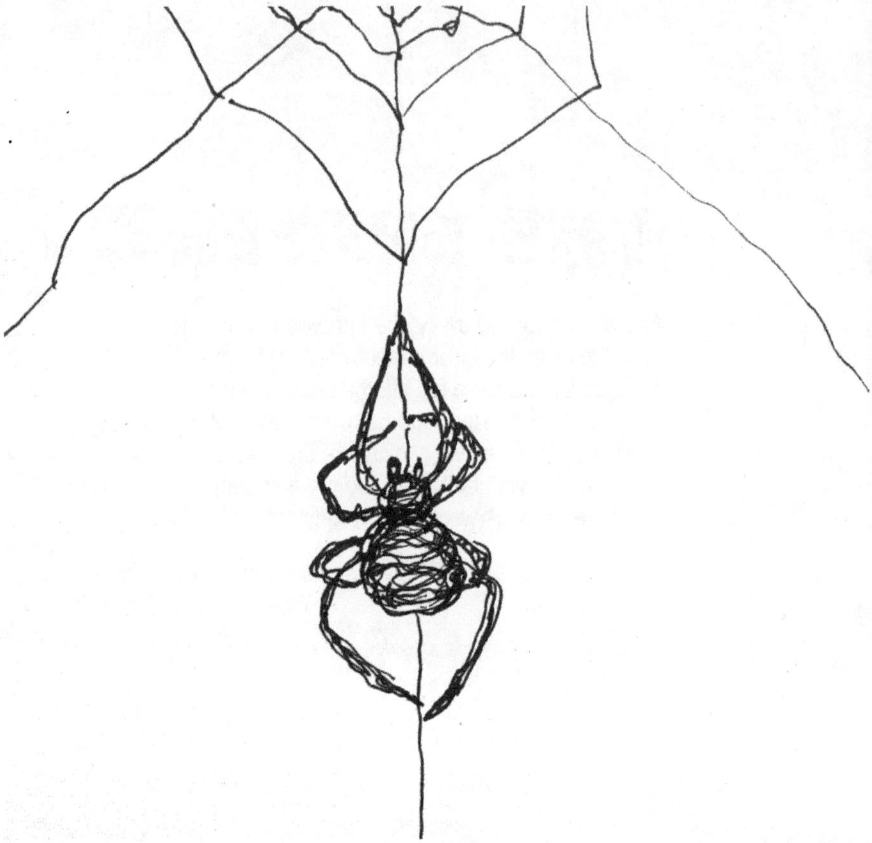

spider: asks

herself why
spider asks
why am I the hangman
why hang myself

upside down on a whim
a thousand thin threads
my life depends on

I try
to speak myself to sleep
and sometimes across
the night silence

the world so long I swing alone
arms empty
the hours tucked under my pendulum
week after week i
swim across canyons & never cross
a soul—do not spot a thing

why do I hang on your every word
the smallest chance of return

spider: gives order

to the universe
spider to flattery grown
increasingly susceptible
in light of such indecencies
and the terrible dehiscence in wind

asks of her own finery
does it give order
to the splayed & flailing waters
the scattered & scalding constellations

has begun to fasten
islands together
with clothes pins
& hook them
on her breath

night & day sashays
across the arms of creation
the ligatures her legs let out
for what is rent
and what is whole

in long-legged zeal
lays correction lines

forever zipping
& unzipping
the fabric she
stitches over the burning
chaos of flies

spider: a climber

whose safety
belt has held

                    a bag of communiqués
                    a salvo of spit

a teardrop spider on
a spindle of runaway DNA

slave to upanddown ways
                    its saliva lethal
more deadly than salvia

alarmed perhaps
to have expressed itself
so openly spider

scuttles up its innards

retracts everything it has said
takes back every word of it

spider: has grown

one leg wound
round high romance
the fabric of her vision
the nights small
packages dumped by the dark

radar is the fastidiousness bred in her
nothing too far or too negligible

she runs
stops
stoops
to the casualties
their blind stumble

meticulously every morning
vacuums the carpet
in exact delicacy wipes up
the detritus of what
has shuddered onto the night

spiders: their jottings

beads they tell
up & down the line
tiny perforations
perorations in time
scratchings on air

their thoughts tighten
balance in ball-
point precision

the water dimples
under their weight

their eight thoughts smolder

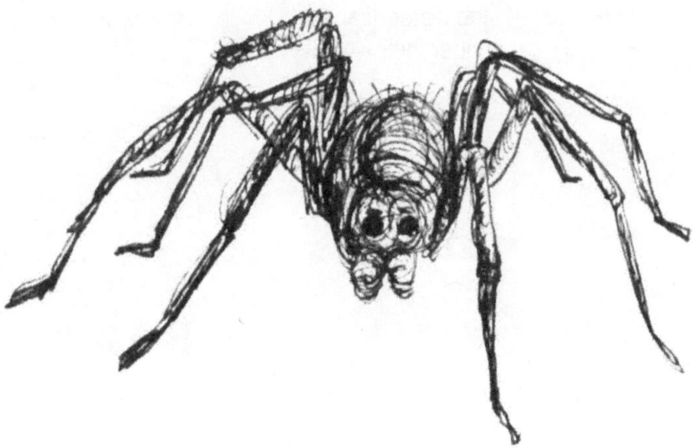

spider: spared

up & down the spokes
up & down the strings
          she begins
the journey perilous

spider has a fine ear
when visitors announce themselves
spider is a good listener
waits for arrivals

on other lines spider is
thoughtful ready to greet
to show the way in
                    throws herself
                        // out for them
                                            admires
          the lines hardening behind her

spider: alone in a western

morning a clear quinine
earth low & horizontal, brooding
the eastern sky long & loping
                                        is tipping
              way out of
whack   squashing everything

                                        imagine her
sequestered in a dusky room
the curtains slow & dusty

she plinks on her piano
time waits & listens
tenses where he feels her
two-stepping two-timing ways

knows her looks
are killing

spider: plays

the leading lady
casts line after line
into the dark spits
into the river

on leggy boots plays
high-lace suspicions

spendthrift spider speeds
up & down the moonlight
flings her lines
tugs them tight and pins
her tent down
for the night yanks
the draw strings shut

in the morning stoops
to inspect the small
jewels in her purse

spider: in Gusterath

climbs into funnels
in the grass &
pops
/out of sight

when he blows on it
a fennel seed
trickles down,
, tumbles
down the throat,
incredulous
as Alice, perfectly
at home , homely,

the Striethorst's yard shaggy
for these parts wild & shaggy as the two
little ones their crazy pell-mell energy
and a tiny spider that tickles at the
rabbit hole

spider: plucky little fellow

their music loves her
                    when they play
12-string & she watches
him strut watches him wave
his bright pedipalp
loves his silent & shining words

       he knows he has to be
          quick with the words

she likes how
          ten   ta
                 tive how fear
                      fully he reaches
                                        out to
                            twang

her threads he chooses
          one side knows
how to brush her in a special way
knows how to touch
as always she has wanted
her strings plinked

he will try to duck
past her welcome
find the smallest opening
whisper inky secrets in her ear

spider: contemplates

old age because it is
an old adage she will teeter on
a goitered existence
wish when the late-night news
unrolls the day she can still feel
the good times
quick and slippery

she would like something more
lasting grows tired of playing
the fat lady does she want
glamour will she clamour for romance

she whose eyes once
shone with neon
fears late at night
the moon has turned
to a milky spud
in a muddy sky

fears she will end up all alone
in gartered boredom
macraméing by moonlight

ARKOLOGY

And they went in unto Noah into the ark, two and two of all flesh, wherein is the breath of life.

—Genesis 7:15

the snail

i.

under its umbrella
oozes   oozes
hauls it
self up &
eases
over shelves

gravely as an old man in a churchyard
more smoothly than an undertaker
over
&
up
drags its shade
a slab of shale
across the gravel

shelters in cold mud
and the wind shoulders past

ii.

in umbrage intact
snail sheds air shreds sun
taking its own sweet time
swigs wetly among
twigs tastes the thin sweet licour
in algae over stones slathers
mucous in its wake
rubs the world to slipperiness

iii.

precarious where everything is
unbuckled unsnapping
the world in water
filled galoshes sloshes
not for love nor for all the love
in the word would it move
to a dryer or less smelly place

the jackfish

the round water
rolls heavily
green & cold

the quick
speckles
filtering

its eyes
golden nitrogen
the lakewater flutters through
the long collar of its throat

gripping
frogs
ripping baby
turtles baby ducks cormorants in its jaws sun
fish pickerel maria whitefish crayfish gold
eye lake trout sucking their perfect flesh

their icicle bones
lodged in its gut

ursula major

a shoulder blade rocks prairie swirls in stink old dam matted hair
the mottled horses her face cut & bites flies fester her eyes whirl
over head ***whhw wwhh whhh*** bright ropes the mares teeth &
eyes her sin being bear bearing prairie in her shamble & shit she
rumbles berries garnets burn forever she runs on all fours across
fire in the far coulees her mind a mat of fear

every fall cowboys on a tear rouse a squall of cubs & dogs flush
them from the smell of spruce their bewildered shambling stand
on shins slice them open in hairy skins people love to dance deep
into roots & berries & ants run them down run them into wire into
snares fire their paws & hides their clumsy panic before wind &
smoke to their shoulders the ticks & warbles horses with mens
heads & shoulders huge flies at their shit

she turns & turns the sun splinters her face dizzy cannot reach
the barbwire necklace they court her with small beads gleam like
sparks & lead her to men of the world adrenaline on their breath
take turns at her they are what rumbles the plains bison light up
small creatures scorched & crushed panic grizzlies black bears
in their stench & flies & love of berries driven to dance in shit &
terror when the stars have frozen and Orion brightly climbs to
constellations full of burnt thistles and embers splash into her will
she dance when they ask her for the last dance will she save it for
them

seam stresses

embroider the water they walk on
their fine and delicate needle-work
pierces the world's skin

tiny mosqui
toes dip their threads
into the river of your breathing

ii.
ii. ii.
, = 0: "... -.
3-. ' 3 , = 0: "... -0: "... -.
3-. 3 3-. 3
1 ,1,,[
1 ,1,,[1 ,1,,[
. ÷ 1 11' . ÷
. ÷ . ÷1 11' 1 11' . ÷ . ÷
- 3.. 3.. 3..
10382 57
10382 57 10382 57
\
\ \
0 \
0 \ 0 \
| +
| + | +
... (... (... (
(: ...
^!)((: !~ (:... ...
^!)(^!~)(!~
~" '+
~" '+ '+

the perfume of your CO_2
brightens their hot wax

your thorax a chimney
through which thoughts pass
blackening on the way out

bee longings

from waxed rooms they
step into the light & brighten
for as Pliny knows the clapping of hands
and the clinking of brass pleases bees

the pungent and blinding
mist of their visits
across the clover and goldenrod
the return to the perfectly shaped pockets

they spend a lot of time in the sauna
adjusting their leggings
sniffing pollen   sipping tea
their gilded motions
ache with blueburning sugar

my father who, no Shortribs, or Sheepshanks,
no Laceleg, yet dreams of surpassing
Rumpelstiltskin, is spinning honey into a tub
smoke buffer huffing in hand and
wrapped in a keeper's unearthly duds
tramples through the long grass and

when he bumps
into the hive

we can hear the terrible longings
shake their bodies
let out a sudden and awful roar

meanwhile pigs

talk they don't
keep much to themselves
their bewhiskered ruminations
on dung & flies

cherish the close and convivial inquiries
join in their songs of chop & dandelions
daily probe the state of turnips
consider with gravitas
the bulge of cabbage

old geezers on the porch
sizing up the neighbours

though genial in patience
the pigs rave and swear
rains will wash over
just you wait
just you wait & see the sun

will surely hit in a splot
sweeter than a slop-pail
full of rotten potatoes

also and not to be pooh-pooed
/the flies
will arrive
in a strange sizzle
a hard lacquer in their gaze

the pigs will grow miscreant
tail-twistingly giddy with all
the guzzling and slurping
crazed with the delicacies
sucking them down
blue flies shiny as candies

death by installment

meanwhile behind the barn
the grasshoppers in gossip
are logging the grass

the sun flickers inside
the snakes slide around eggs
the hens have hidden in the hay

in the house the flies
are buzzing the kitchen
scouting for a place to land

a loose heart

they rub and bang
against the ship's wooden ribs
wait like an egg to happen

the bright moon fills
the months
stains a blue-linen sky

in a cold green
garden they call the North
West Passage beluga
whales swallow China whole
tons of green tea sluice
plankton thicker than leaves

a symphony of wind & strings
or so they seem
their musings

you can hear
the blueness of their bodies
8 octaves blue
whales 1600 miles
their long keening
could be mourning
the end of the world

raccoon poet
(for george bowering)

the safe-cracker tenderness
in your eyes   & your hands   george
you feel   softly
on soft hands   & soft feet dance

brush skimmilk fingers over keys
as if panning for gold
and with them cover your grievous ears & eyes

reckless commando from strange lands
fling yourself from fence to
the neighbour's raspberry patch
swing from a rope no one can see
face first into the toilet bowl
poke your black and shining face into everything

having all this
going for you george
you hero with a thousand faeces
why do you gorge your face

this is egregious george
why do you do this
make tracks all over the page

why do you play with your gorgeous tail
why do you still
oh bower of bliss george i am
curious   this is   what
i want   to know
:: puddle around
in your own ring of piss

the wasps

sh >oul der »¥ »» sar ms

Vha nds H ö}d E

ad»ne ¥ck

ne ¥-cks- (((haö}d ndsÖ}d ha nö}dds

ho ±ulde Ĥ rs! a *rm* sha ?nd <she a,d

hea ö}dnec} K shou[l ders

ou ¿**ou** lders! **ou** ¿**ou** ld

ers! **ou**

¿**ou** lders! ar ~~msh~~ and**s**ha ndshe a ±

± dne ; **ou** ¿**ou** lders! ar Ÿms

msm-sm.sms.m

gila

hear the humming
birds at their hovering
moving in intricate calculus
colour and pattern

the long hollow tube
sounds issue from
they know it is her
arrived from the
nectar of the desert
the music of her
feeding

Australia

"In one summer, there it was.
Bulrushes, weeds, flowers, shrimps, the
whole bit, and at night we'd hear a few
frogs going away at it, like baying at the
moon."

if storms were to hit
where heat moves like welts in sand

would something in you dissolve
and the cracks close up

shrimp spinning madly
fish unsnap from the salt ponds
and the cormorants glut on the rush

that's when flat little frogs shrug off
the bags they've slept years in
tug night shirts over
heads and bright flowers
billions of seeds let go in a racket

this is possible
where birds breed on shore
a place where sand & clay & six
foot lizards smash snakes
& rains sweep away
the salt and silt

you yourself could be
a hot sudden lake in the world
making sounds
of drains unclogging
sounds koalas make in mating

benny

they call him as if in
benediction, or benefaction,
wwhh wwhw whhwh
and he perks
one a benny, two a benny
the voice, the whistle
the summons from winter

hears from where he has
stored last year
the scrape of door
the rattle of seeds & nuts

answers in scoots
the face which he has learned
to know and meet

the trust of a remembered life
brings his soft quick body, in squirts,
tiny hands to large creatures that
in neighbourly voices
call and whistle

a sparrow dips

a saucer of light vaughan might say
within whose eye the eye of sun
in sand or powder runs
and in april drips

snow at the feeder
a sparrow dips
small swivel of bones
bone to bone brought
on invisible thread

a string from mandel's store
a button they spun christmas on

they are all gone
into the world of light
he said

mar 21, morning

fat-bodied flat-footed
two geese bugling
two long necks pumping
non-stop from the roof
sennet to this
our goodly earth

the hot tar and gravel to which
from ditch and marsh and slough
they have risen wide as their own feet
on which they will raise themselves
and a colony of themselves
the latest iteration of roof-dwellers

this is ours their voices declaim
this roof is ours this noble plain
to which from ditch and marsh
we have in regency ascended

and so also these rubber feet
that slap against the summer heat
our tar our gravel our ledge
our view through the wide windows
where the coffee drinkers live

this gander's mine this goose is mine
we two together be in one
and this our noble house
this ledge our demesne

their clangour insufficient
they drop like reluctant bombers
run in long-necked
hisses at a young male
who lingers by the big slab of limestone

once safe he sings softly to himself
gathers against his heaviness and
lifts across the parking lot
past St. Andrews until he
turns into the vast and widening west

that afternoon two lone males
les arrivistes loitering beside the College

the older one, bigger, shoulders
toward the smaller guy who sidles away
yuh yuh yuh he says, the bigger one
yuh yuh yuh

they will leave
turds that look a lot
like dead black slugs
or kids' licorice plugs
one end touched
deceptively gray
as if smoldering with desire

the slug

had dragged itself
down
the cement steps
through the
large german doorway

a long vapour trail
across the tile

collapsed in
a wake of cellophane

groundhog

first alarm when the neighbour arrives
he's friendly enough, pleasant actually,
but you can tell something is up
when he hurries his middle-linebacker frame
across the driveway into the yard closes fast
on the step stops to peer as if he sees there
a fullback waiting for a draw play

turns out he has cornered our friendly ground hog
who has borrowed a home under the step
and having shrugged off his shadow ambles the yard
hangs around to watch our daughters come and go
greets me when over the stones i arrive
chunky creature ready to sprawl
splat on his stomach
for ceremony of sun and the love of company
sheer pleasure in a corner of summer
just past the wild allium
that smells sharply of onion
when the mail carrier arrives to find him
splayed on the step

neighbour alarmed that the fat little guy
would tunnel like a sapper under his house
blow it possibly in one monstrous explosion or,
more likely, drag it slowly into the clay that clogs
the bottom of Lake Agassiz

middle-aged linebacker instincts intact
scourge now of a fat little guy who wants
only to lie in the sun

Évora

The first day. Dusk. He, excited, points.
Look at those birds. Swallows, they must be swallows. The skim & veer. Barn swallows on the prairies, they say.
Granaries that smell of mice.

They drink insects. They have to swallow their words, whole.
Swel, the dictionary says, they swel down their food.

In Évora swallows move like minnows, swim the blinding Portuguese sky. The air flushes over them and they dip into the hollows, wallow on wind.

Make homes of earth & water.

Next day, leaving, stop to
straighten their backs, squint, and
it's come down with mumps, the building,
a line of clumps along the wall

going in & out, swift zippers
flickers in the city's throat.

flights shut down

May 11/04

sparrow its quick
small bones
crumb to crumb

turns to gummy streaks
what's left of spilled coffee?
scrapes its small beak
down its stomach
rubs through the spill

away and back
more needle gouging
          more rubbing
throat & stomach

jump-flies to chair
scrapes its beak
in the round holes

     back & forth
fuzz-headed and pecking

next morning wet
snow over everything
the cedar broken and
all the birds calling

a wild turkey
sentinel on the fence

adam and eve again

he said:
you do not love god's creatures

she said:
i can't stand the ratty things

he said:
look how they arrive through the dazzling snow
stirring up puffs in their run down the fence
how they hurry to the rattle
jump softly up on the table
hold peanuts in their small soft hands
how quickly they open and chew them

look how they leap onto
the squirrel-proof feeder
bounce from its deep-slanted snow
onto the basket of suet
swing in triumph
taste the sweetness of life

watch how they leap across the sky
to feeder to bar slippery bar to bar
swing in loops and parabolas
onto the green metal post
wring themselves round one turn
and the other turn themselves
inside out upside down slide up
the shepherd's crook
shake off mere gravity
hook themselves round
more quickly than monkeys

do you not see how
against a skinny winter
they shinny up and down
suspend their hunger where they shine
and stand in the air on their heads
suck down sunflower seeds
ripened in mennonite fields

you must have noticed them
fling themselves four feet up
through the bright air
into a basket of peanuts
appointed to the jays

look where they stand
up on their legs
hold their small hands
prayerfully before them devout
as an anglican divine

peer hopefully through the patio door
to the source of manna
i am waiting to pour
into their cold snowy winter

she said:

i don't like them
they are ugly
they look like rats

The Sparrow Syllogisms

Opinion On The Topic:
sparrows are nice

Argument Against Your Opinion:
sparrows shit on everything

Reason Supporting Your Opinion:
they are chirpy

Another Reason Supporting Your Opinion:
sparrows eat everything

3rd Reason Supporting Your Opinion (optional):
they have lots of energy

Option 1:
Even though sparrows shit on everything, sparrows are nice because they are chirpy and sparrows eat everything.

Option 2:
While sparrows shit on everything, they are chirpy.

Option 3:
Sparrows shit on everything because sparrows eat everything.

Option 4:
Some people argue that sparrows shit on everything even though it's a well-known fact that sparrows are nice, they are chirpy, sparrows eat everything, and they have lots of energy.

Option 5:
Even though sparrows are nice people argue that sparrows shit on everything.

Option 6:
Sparrows shit on everything because sparrows eat everything.

a nag

, a snag

a mag
pie friend
tries haggling for three-toed love
niggling for the smallest bit
says *pica pica*
pica pica

crow cannot figure is it smirk or snigger
crow himself leans on strut & swagger
gnaws on the world's shoulder
wagers everything on bluff

meanwhile mag pie is trying
a new tact another word a new ward
robe he's long been fancying
a magician's cape a country
singer's snazzy duds
something smarter than a tux

"These birds love to utter certain words
which they not only learn but are fond of
and ponder carefully. . . It is generally
held that if they are defeated by the
difficulty of a word, they die . . . and that
when they are searching for a word,
they cheer up miraculously if they hear
it." (Pliny 147)

Mag pie chirrups with her eight friends
nitter nitter she says
pica pica they say

turncoat birds   they say *tut tut*
till crow who wanted to swoosh & thunder
splendid as king tut
finds himself down on his luck
down on his knees begging

to be forgiven
to be let in
on the secret

what's he know
magpie the fortune bird
good news bird

where on earth can crow
get a vest like that

the oyster

in due season oysters open
their mouths and the dew stirs
roundness into them

when they come to fullness
the shells release
a sour nectar gives
rise to a cloudy issue
the unsullied dew
emanates bright clear ones
pleasing to the eye and hand

if properly treated they grow
well and truly yet in neglect
they change colour

if assailed by hail and lightning the shells
close up and they shrink to kidney stones
so also thunder irks the oysters
who shut so suddenly
they produce "wind" pebbles
in disappointment shrug off
swollen and feeble things

healthy pearls tuck in
to the soft folds and begin to form
underwater they feel
soft feel safe

when touched they make a fist
when a shell feels a hand
it snaps shut as if stricken
it holds on tight
and won't let go
if the hand persists
it bites so hard it cuts it off

no two of them alike
in size and radiance and shape
in texture and rich in colour
each of them only themselves

—adapted from John F. Healy's translation of *Pliny the Elder: Natural History: A Selection*

startled you on LeMay

when you opened
the cedar gate to the afternoon
: : :

a strange fat creature
big hairless guy on his bum
on the edge of the yard
utterly unperturbed and staring
back as if he had been expecting you
as if he were about to confide or confer
as if he were sitting at the pub with you

has risen from the cool
earth to the chumminess of day
he might swim and bathe in
feet dangling stubbily over the ledge
hedging his bets on neighbourliness

and the other little guy
years later on Pasadena
the sky on its back splayed
contently on the driveway
happy as a tea cosy

they pledged themselves
against eviction
the two of them
two convivial hedgehogs
one big / one small
two round lumps warming with sun

crooners

> "Homer did not describe the sirens, name them, or give their lineage. Many later writers identified them as daughters of [. . .] Muses, and said that they were winged women with bird feet or else birds with women's heads and voices."—Edward Tripp, *The Meridian Handbook of Classical Mythology*

i.

it is obvious that cows try to look
like boulders and closely to imitate rusting cars
grow intimate among the grass & posts
ruminant with stinkweed

near as they can when you
blow by east of dusk
country music on the radio
strong wind at the back

if you listen closely if you
open your ears
or your door
you can
hear them
by the ditches
by the fences
,breathing

a faint lowing when time swishes
around and through them

everyone can hear the softness of their calls

ii.

a few dawdle, muster
all the dignity they can manage
they are Dutchees and they
gather majestically
in mustard splotches

unperturbed by the ditches filling
with bones and bottles and beetles
they know the mysteries of grass & wind
remember when the skies roll over
they move amiably inside and
curiosity nudges them to the fences

they croon to passing trucks
pull over they sing pull
over their liquid eyes
and slow bone amble say
they are keeping
watch plowing air

they want to scratch the moon
soothe the shaggy & unpastured wind

watch as it washes over them
and they sing, sending
their breathing out
through the doorsills
and the nostrils of the world

magpie

> They had to become new birds within the forest,
> And as they tried to beat their breasts, their wings
> Were black, their bodies swung midair. They were
> Gossips in trees yet all had human voices—
> A fearful noise, they talk, talk, talk forever.
> —Ovid, *The Metamorphoses*, Book V. Trans. Horace Gregory.

black-billed thick-willed
thief with an awfully long tail
and an excellent sense of smell
not to be confused
with the false magpie, treepie

not a simple black and white
for he proudly wears
iridescence upon his back
and all year sticks around

in vengeance against drab and duff
scavenges odd-shaped stones
polished sticks and broken bones
seeks among beetles and grass
hoppers worms and moles
ticks and nuts and seeds
also eggs and pet food

mostly walking, now and
then hopping, sometimes skipping
hoping for shine or glisten
talks and chitters with friends
and with himself

raider of caches scratches his head
gathers where he can bright-faced foil
hopes for buckles & buttons & coins he can lug off
to woo his lady sprinkles ants over himself
selects with the skill of a jeweler
spoons cigarette lighters the reds and yellows
and blue things that perk in the sun

pieces that pierce his eye old voler
he fields tape stashes candy wrappers
rummages string to tie up his trinkets
and he steals away home

admires what piques or pleases
sets aside and buffs with his breath
until he has mirrors in which he
can almost see himself

യാക്ക യാക്ക he says യാക്ക യാക്ക
beckons to his love
hopes to set
the molecules jingling

it's Abigail they named her

how perfect says Mrs. B.
at least it ain't Anita
it ain't Esmeralda
she ain't no prefect
she ain't no perfect
she ain't behavin'

and who could blame her
brought into abnegation
no saint she knows
        nothing is easy
        everything tainted
the sour and unreasonable weather
the sky a tub drained of colour

grown gaunt on ruminations
the hard denial of flesh
the poke around her neck
the fence in sharp reproof
the wire against ambling

wishes under a hopped-up
moon to decamp and light out
the fence shaking & trailing
        snakily behind

DNA yanking her away
Abigail in a slather climbs
a wobbly ladder to heaven on which crow
hikes his robes & holds court

knows what there is to be
smelled in the neighbour's ravine
snuffing of the neighbour's bull
every scent and succulence on the other side
something of the heart's discontent

nothing for her hereabouts
but barbs & thistles
epistles & curtains
nothing but abnegation

a crimp in our dreams too
for us it is certain
there can be no more
oozing with milk &
honey no more
joy at the end of
a fully appointed rainbow

an angry god flames in the sky
and the sun is at hand
a pestle he hones & grinds
rain to alkali   us to leather

so dry we sweat only salt
substance to poison the wells
blight the beds we wish to lie in

love in the wilds

(of Banff):

both male and female
made he them then
came they two
by two two by two and fur by careful

: The Elk
fear by four elk can charge at any who knows
time be especially what you
alert spry chirpy ani   might scare
mated wake full sprightly fore up or what
warned during mating   might change

season and calving
time some know
elk that get out
(of hand) have been
tagged or marked
do not be offended
do not be off-handed

please be
careful if you can if you N
counter or chant an elk with these signs

signs of a dangerous
elk which shall be
to all those who have
not lost their head head held
high teeth exposed
ears back

makes direct eye
contact with whites
of eyes showing if
you are feeling
uneasy get be

hind a tree or any
large object you
should above & below
all avoid a skirmish
a run-in a set-to more
than anything a show-down

do not take uncalled
-for chances or advantages
we are talking risk, eh?

: Cougars

Cougars are not often seen
(in these or any parts) because
they are solitary
elusive and active mainly
at night you can help

avoid a brush
with a cougar
by travelling in a large
group and making
lots of noise if you run

into a cougar face
the animal and retreat
slowly be sure you leave

an escape route
an out a way out
for the cougar do
not run or play

dead try to appear
bigger by holding
your arms up or
an object shout wave
your arms a large
stick back

and forth throwing
rocks may deter
an attack if approached
be firm fight
back

: Bears
Who's afraid of?
Be Aware Of: Walk
with your head

up and look
around often when
hiking make a commotion call

out or raise
your voice big
racket wouldn't hurt

you have to face it
the bears know you
are there it is
best to take a hike

in a bunch carry
spray and watch
for signs of
a bear a bear

may be in the area in
dications of
activity include torn
up logs turned over rocks tracks
and scat it is time to scat to
light out and leave
the area if the signs look
fresh if ever you should
come across

a large dead animal leave
the area immediately and report

to Comm
Unity Sir
Vices stay

calm if you cross
paths with a bear do not

alarm the bear with screams or sudden
movements try not to be up
set calm be
haviour will reassure
the bear do not make eye

contact looking
deep into heirs eye
may get the dander
up get your spray
ready using slow
movements speak in a gentle
and quiet voice back

away slowly always
elude side-step slide
-step evade never
take on never
run be prepared
for a bluff charge
or "woofing" it is diff i

cult but import ant to remain
still at this critical stage any
un-X pecked it move
meant may pro

voke any bear you hit upon
   and so you should
         guard against in
-your-face behavi our
 if you do catch
      the bear's eye
                              lie face
              down with arms
behind your neck and legs
                       apart it is time

to grin and bare it if
         the overt ures last
gladly the bear id cross
                          eyed bear
         more than a few

minutes begin fighting
                          back do not
let the bear think
you are a push-over
let the bear know you

                                   are not easy
                                   pray please
   help us keep
the animals wild

iii-nn thuh bleewwww-Kuh-
NAY-Dee-uhn-RAW-keys

THE BIRDS

Totototototototototototinx,
Tio, tio, tio, tio, tiotinx!
—Aristophanes, *The Birds,*
acting edition prepared by Walter Kerr.

feeders

you got to put it so
the birds can see it
a long ways off

you dont
they feel
: boxed in

they need to size things up
you know
or else they wont come

when theyre approaching
same thing : they have to see
they can get away

once theyre there
they just go crazy
: sing their heads off

being exposed thats what
theyre worried about
getting caught when theyre
not looking or cant see

theyre checking & peeking &
all the time watching & bobbing

if they cant
they up
&
fly off

the criminal immensities of love

i.

night shrugs
off the navy peacoat
tosses morning aside

ii.

winter dumps itself
hissing into the sun

& the birds fall
from the rafters
the nests and noise
whiffle into corners
onto cantilevered winds
over water in elm & willow
near brow and elbow

iii.

robins begin to twitch
in runs & hops
bump their shadows
before them

iv.

baltimore orioles hang & drip
little lemons
on evergreens burn
brighter than
christmas trees

swallows in their porches
and finches in small bright
buttons pinched off

v.

pigeons peer sideways
smirk at the pasty
whiteness of your passion

oriole

o
ori
oles
threa
ded the
dark ness
into a round
sock hung it in a
tree rolled the sun
in sat on it until they
turned bright yellow
orioles the roles
they played

the heron

balances
- beautifully
could be carved from shale

a killer on stilts
stalking fish and frogs
stands in water until

it becomes a tree   becomes shelter

except it looks   almost out of fettle
so taken with the shallows   it seems

tipsy   with its own shadow
off-kilter in love   with itself
in the water

hard knuckle of its skull
a comedy of hood and hunch
settles into dream
its second self   sleeps in its height

swallows its own darkness   its quiet
waits to   breathe   the quick minnows

crouches its whole life
under an umbra of wings   /waits
to stab
to run
over the water
splashingly
after itself

the jays

arrive every morning
an hour past dawn
at first one
sometimes only one
on the fence
/watches

a rattle of peanuts
/a flash of blue
to paving stones
table
basket

this one & then
this one
& then

this one the jay
dropping
them one by
one
bounces on its toes

a watch maker's inspection
testing, testing, two,
four, sometimes five before
back to the first &
a swift burst
into the spruce

more & more swatches
more & more picking
what length what thickness
will do which nubs suffice
an exquisite measuring
examines bends & dents
weighs knobs & warts until

/one works

rain slashes

the lightning   shatters
the shutters   smack

the hail   clatters
the aspens   shudder
the eaves troughs   splash

a small flying machine
skitters & jerks
across your front
lawn across the dandelions

a cold stubby fuse
it sputters
a blurry red
in the rain

it shifts & sings
worryworry
when it spots you

littoral, june

the yard glows marmalade
birds work the edges
like watchful nurses
robins black birds grackles circle

SHH SSHH SHH
the sprinkler a bright mandala
loudly counsels discretion

despite which
robins with rusted breasts wait and
baby jays drink but do not douse
their stubby blue flames

and grackles, cuffs pulled
to their knees, arrive like angry clerics

water *flipflipflip*
brings them
they lunge open-faced
gulp the wet worms the red
headed woodpecker shares

a glass flute
/ a grey
jay
& another
a gate opening in its throat

blackbirds from a dry summer
mosey into the yard
their speckled babies
almost unrecognizable
before sun
burns them black

bittern

a basket of wool & needles
teeters on horny legs
drops the dank & drooling shadows

the marshes a green sneeze
shine like nickels

fish on its breath it leans
tracing in the water
your quicksilver dreams

grackles

it begins
innocently enough

a squalor of fog
a stupor of frogs

wishing for mist & little jars of rain
waiting for a squall they can slog through
ditches thick with snails and smells

and then
/skirmishers
/grackles
fan out and swagger
stab their eyes into the ground

shoulder toward the sprinkler
threaten to sideswipe the robins
who flee with their premonitions

big-bully storm troopers
their metal iridescence
straight as stukas toward august

the blackbird

sing tossing
the blackbird morning

unlocks the blockaded light
unbraids the yellow air

streaks the bearded sun
the avalanche of wind

blowing the cat-tails stiff
the brocade sheared-off

the black bird berates
the winds beat and scrape

chevron on its shoulders
wet with blood